s a differentiated text version of
Detective Investigates Victorian Crime
hrisp

first published in 2009 by Wayland

© Wayland 2009

hildren's Books
Road
/1 3BH

stralia
Kent Street
V 2000

ng Editor: Jennifer Sanderson
ine Wilkinson
Hayley Fairhead

y Cataloguing in Publication Data
z
rime. - Differentiated ed. -
ry detective)
Great Britain - History - 19th century -
rature
hrisp, Peter
034

502 5705 3

na

division of Hachette Children's Books,
UK Company.
livre.co.uk

Picture acknowledgements:

The publishers would like to thank the following for
permission to reproduce their pictures:
BEAMISH The North of England Open Air Museum
14 (right), 16 (right), 17 (bottom-left); Billie Love
Historical Collection 19 (bottom), 23 (top), 25
(bottom), 27 (top), 27 (bottom); Bridgeman Art
Library cover (bottom-left, middle, bottom-right,
top-right); John Frost 28; Hulton Getty 22; Jim
Linley/Inverary Jail 27 (right); Mary Evans Picture
Library cover (top-left), 1, 4, 5 (left and right), 7, 8
(bottom), 9, 11, 12 (left and right), 13 (left), 14 (top),
15 (bottom), 17 (top and right), 18 (top-left and top-
right), 19 (left), 20 (right), 21, 23 (bottom), 25 (top-
left), 26, 29 (top and bottom); Museum of London
cover (rattle); Peter Newark's Pictures 10 (left and
right), 13 (bottom), 15 (top), 16, 19 (top-right), 24;
Punch 6; Ronald Grant Archive 8 (top).

Note:

The website addresses included in this book were
valid at the time of going to press. However,
because of the nature of the Internet, it is possible
that some addresses may have changed, or sites
may have changed or closed down since
publication. While the authors and Publishers regret
any inconvenience this may cause the readers, no
responsibility for any such changes can be accepted
by either the author or the Publishers.

**Be a
History
Detective**

Victoriar
Crime

Liz Gogerly

WAYLAND

This book
The History
by Peter C

This editior

Copyright

Wayland
Hachette C
338 Euston
London NW

Wayland Au
Level 17/207
Sydney NSV

Commission
Designer: Elc
Proofreader:

British Librar
Gogerly, Li
Victorian c
(Be a histo
1. Crime -
Juvenile lite
I. Title II. C
364.9'41'09

ISBN: 978 0 7

Printed in Ch

Wayland is a
an Hachette
www.hachette

Contents

Words in **bold** can be found in the glossary.

Victorian Crime

The Victorian era was a time of change. Millions of people moved from the countryside to towns and cities. The population grew. In 1837 there were 16 million people in Britain. By 1901 there were 37 million people. There was more crime than ever before.

Slums

Poor people lived in the worst parts of towns and cities. These dirty, overcrowded areas were called **slums**. People in the slums often had to steal money or food to live.

▲ *Join the history detective, Sherlock Bones, and investigate Victorian crime!*

Look out for Sherlock's paw-prints – each one has a mystery for you to solve. The answers are on pages 30–31.

❂ Why do you think this slum was called 'the devil's acre'?

Crime and the poor

Middle-class Victorians blamed the poor for crime. In the cartoon on the right, crime is a scary phantom. The phantom comes from the slums.

Face of a criminal

Some middle-class Victorians thought criminals looked like apes. In the cartoon below, the criminals have wide mouths, small noses and low foreheads.

Jack the Ripper

In 1888, five women were killed in the slums of East London. The murderer was nicknamed Jack the Ripper. The police never caught him.

✿ Why do you think this policeman is wearing a blindfold?

Detective work

Look on the Internet for clues about Victorian crime. Search for other Victorian cartoons. Can you spot more 'criminal faces'?

Who were the 'family people'?

▼ *Criminals often sold their stolen goods to a **fence**. The fence ran a business such as a second-hand clothes shop. The goods were then sold in the shop.*

Some people made a living from crime. It was like their job. These criminals were proud of what they did. They thought they belonged to one big family and so called themselves 'family people'. They called those people who obeyed the law 'outsiders'.

A secret language

Criminals had their own secret language. They could speak without outsiders knowing what they meant. This language was called **cant**. These are some of the canting terms they used:

billy	a silk handkerchief
chiv	a knife
crow	a lookout
crusher	a policeman
flying the blue pigeon	stealing lead off roofs
hoisting	shoplifting
in lavender	hiding from the police
nibbed	arrested
nommus!	get away quick!

▲ *Criminals often met in pubs they called* **'flash houses'**. *This group of criminals is meeting in a flash house in South London.*

☙ What do you think is happening at this flash house?

☙ What do you think this Victorian thief is talking about? Use the words on page 6 to help you.

"We were hoisting billies when our crow spotted a crusher and shouted 'nommus!'"
A Victorian thief

Detective work

Try to find more Victorian canting terms. Look on the Internet. Find words in slang dictionaries. Then try writing your own sentences in cant.

Children and crime

Poor Victorian children often turned to crime. Small boys worked for burglars. They wriggled through barred windows. Then they opened the door for the burglars to get inside. Picking pockets was another common crime for children.

◀ *The Artful Dodger in a film version of* Oliver Twist *from 1948.*

Detective work

What can you find out about child pickpockets? A good place to start is a book by Charles Dickens called *Oliver Twist*. In this story a poor boy becomes a pickpocket.

Pickpockets

Children were good at picking pockets because they were small. They were just the right height to reach a pocket. Often they could snatch a handkerchief or purse without being seen.

▼ *Pickpockets worked in gangs. The gang was run by an adult called a 'kidsman'.*

✿ Read about the Artful Dodger (see below). How can you tell he is poor?

In *Oliver Twist*, there is a pickpocket called the Artful Dodger. Dickens describes him:

"He was a snub-nosed, flat-browed, common-faced boy … short of his age: with rather bow legs, and little sharp ugly eyes…"

A Transfer of Property.

Daring dippers

Pickpockets were also called dippers. When dippers grew older and better at stealing they often stuck to one kind of crime. Some pickpockets robbed passengers on crowded buses. They were called 'maltoolers'. Others dressed as gentleman. They did not look like thieves so people did not suspect them.

▲ *Pickpockets often worked in pairs. The boy on the far left was called a 'stickman'.*

❖ What is the boy on the right trying to do?

❖ How did the 'stickman' help the pickpocket?

Did crime ever pay?

Criminals who robbed banks and broke in to rich people's houses made a lot of money. These criminals were called **cracksmen**. Successful cracksmen often lived and dressed like gentlemen. They only had to do a few big crimes each year. These 'jobs' took months to plan.

▼ *These bank robbers are dressed like gentlemen.*

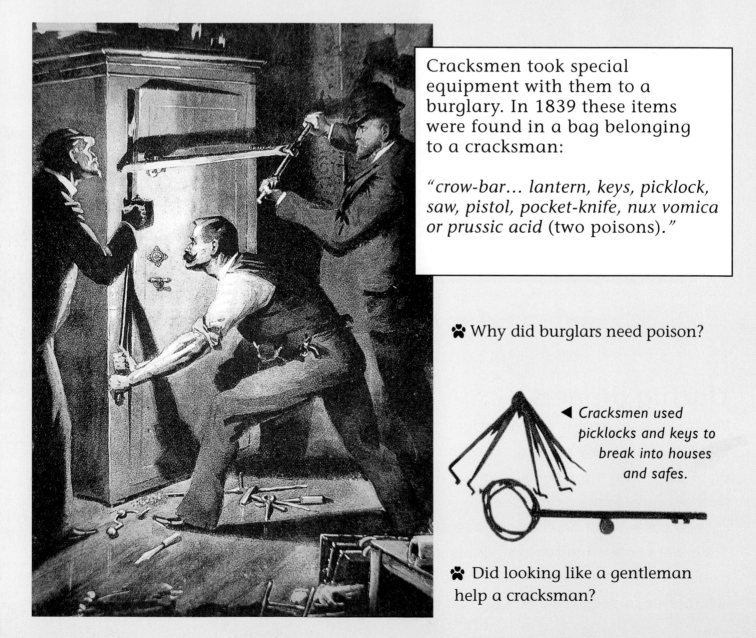

Cracksmen took special equipment with them to a burglary. In 1839 these items were found in a bag belonging to a cracksman:

"crow-bar... lantern, keys, picklock, saw, pistol, pocket-knife, nux vomica or prussic acid (two poisons)."

❖ Why did burglars need poison?

◀ *Cracksmen used picklocks and keys to break into houses and safes.*

❖ Did looking like a gentleman help a cracksman?

The Great Train Robbery

The biggest and most daring robbery of Victorian times was the 'Great Train Robbery'. On 15 May 1855, Edward Agar and his partner William Pierce robbed the London to Folkestone train. They stole 100 kilograms of gold from a **safe** on the train.

Crime pays

Agar and Pierce were eventually arrested for the crime. At the trial, Agar admitted he had been a thief for over 20 years. In that time, he had never been caught and tried for his crimes. So, for a long time crime did pay for Edward Agar.

▶ *This is a portrait of Edward Agar, who took part in the 'Great Train Robbery'.*

Detective work

If you were Edward Agar, how would you plan to rob a train? What problems would you expect?

The garotters

In 1862, newspapers reported a violent new crime. Burglars were attacking their victims in the streets. They grabbed the victim round the neck and choked them. Meanwhile, another burglar took the victim's belongings. The newspapers called this crime garotting.

✤ This cartoon is from 1862. Why do you think these men are standing back-to-back?

▲ A gentleman is garotted in a dark street. Garotting made some people panic and they stopped going out at night. Other people formed special groups to catch the garotters.

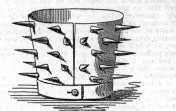

DO YOU WISH TO AVOID BEING STRANGLED!!

If so, try our Patent Antigarotte Collar, which enables Gentlemen to walk the streets of London in perfect safety at all hours of the day or night.

THESE UNIQUE ARTICLES OF DRESS

Are made to measure, of the hardest steel, and are warranted to withstand the grip of

THE MOST MUSCULAR RUFFIAN IN THE METROPOLIS,

Who would get black in the face himself before he could make the slightest impression upon his intended victim. They are highly polished and

Elegantly Studded with the Sharpest Spikes,

Thus combining a most *recherché* appearance with perfect protection from the murderous attacks which occur every day in the most frequented thoroughfares. Price 7s. 6d., or six for 40s.

WHITE, CHOKER, AND Co.

EFFECT OF THE ANTIGAROTTE COLLAR ON A GARROTTEER.

Beating the garotters

In 1863, the government brought in a new law. People who were found guilty of garotting were flogged. This meant they were beaten with a whip. Garotters were also sent to jail.

▲ *A prisoner is flogged at Newgate Prison.*

> ## Detective work
>
> Visit a library that has copies of Victorian newspapers. Look for the *Illustrated London News* and *Punch*. Search for stories and cartoons about crime. Can you find any stories that try to frighten the readers?

🐾 Look at this advertisement for an anti-garotting collar. Do you think it is a serious advertisement?

A poem from *Punch* magazine in 1862.

All around my neck,
I wear a spiked steel collar,
A revolver and a bowie-knife
I carry up my sleeves,
And if any one should ask of
me the reason why I wear them,
I'll tell him 'tis to guard myself
from these garotting thieves.

Poison murderers

In Victorian times, it was not always easy to know how a person died. Sometimes, doctors could not tell the difference between death from poisoning or natural causes. Poison was easy to buy, so murderers often poisoned their victims.

FATAL FACILITY; OR, POISONS FOR THE ASKING.

▲ This cartoon shows how even a child could buy poison from a chemist's shop.

Detective work

Find out about other well-known Victorian poisoners, such as Madeleine Smith, William Palmer and Mrs Florence Maybrick. The Internet is a good place to start your search.

Wicked woman

One of the most famous Victorian murderers was a woman. Mary Ann Cotton probably poisoned 20 people, including four husbands and eight children. Her victims drank tea in which she had put **arsenic**, a deadly poison. She killed them so she could get **insurance money**. She was hanged for her crimes in 1873.

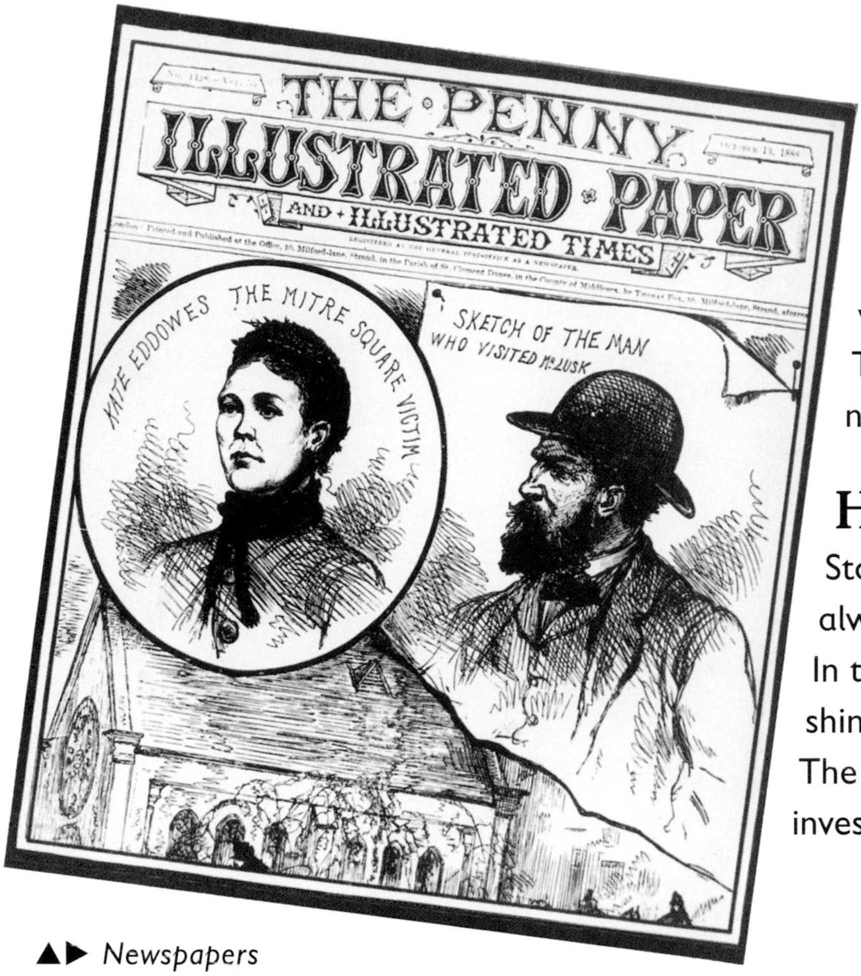

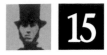

Read all about it!

The Victorians liked to read about shocking murders. Newspapers were filled with stories about crime. These kinds of stories still sell newspapers today.

Helping the criminals

Stories in the newspapers did not always help to catch the criminals. In the cartoon below, a journalist is shining a light on the detective's work. The criminal is reading about the police investigation in the newspaper.

▲▶ *Newspapers ran lots of stories about the murderer Jack the Ripper. He was never caught.*

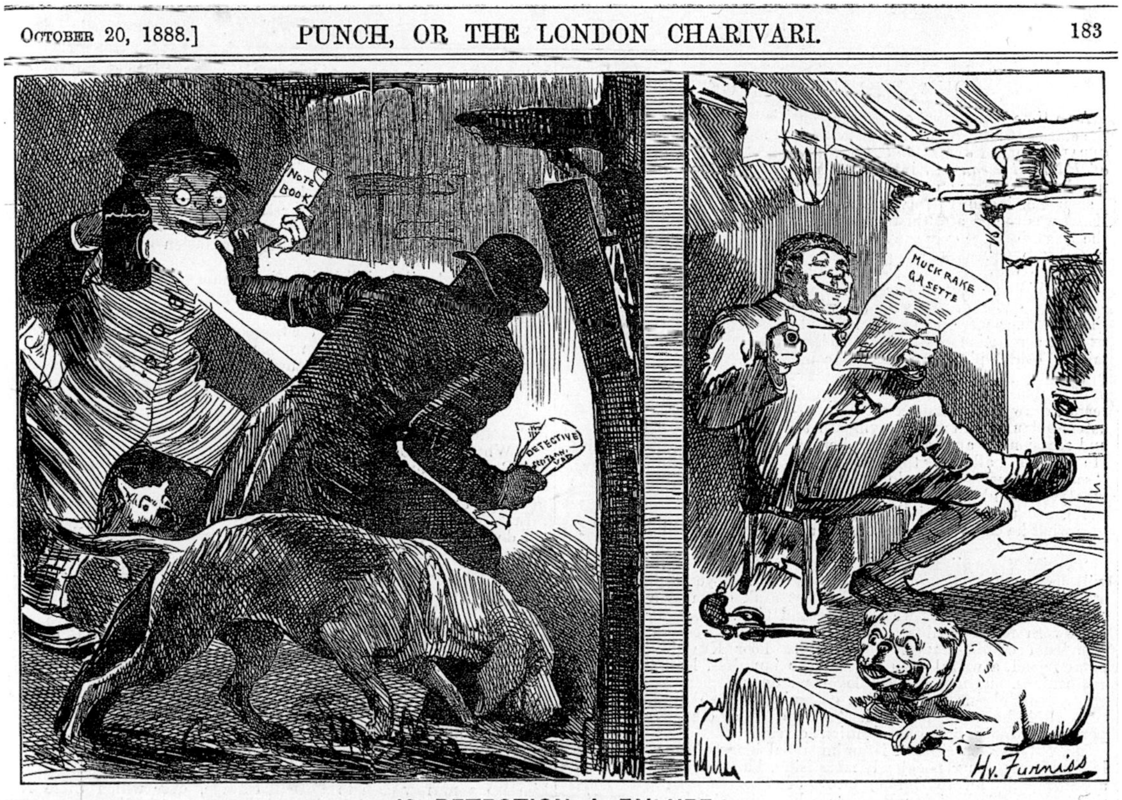

IS DETECTION A FAILURE?

🐾 Why do you think stories in the newspaper helped the criminal?

What was a 'peeler'?

The first police force was started in Victorian times. In 1829, the home secretary of Britain, Sir Robert Peel, set up the London Metropolitan Police Force. The policemen were nicknamed 'bobbies' and 'peelers' after Peel. The new policemen were so good that other police forces were set up all over the country.

Boys in blue

Policemen wore blue coats with brass buttons. They wore blue trousers and black top hats. Each policeman carried a wooden truncheon, handcuffs and a rattle to call for help. The uniform was like servant's clothes. This was because policemen served the public.

> "*They were* [sic] *swallow-tail blue coats, with bright metal buttons... In lieu* [instead of] *of helmets they had an ordinary chimney-pot hat*".
> Edmund Yates, 1885

✿ Why do you think policemen wore top hats?

On the beat

The police caught criminals and stopped crimes from happening. They did this by patrolling the streets. The area they patrolled was called 'the beat'. During one shift a policeman often walked up to 40 kilometres. The police were not popular in the slums. People thought they were there to protect the rich.

✿ Why do you think the police started wearing helmets instead of top hats?

Detective work

The West Midland Police Museum has lots of interesting information, artefacts and photographs from Victorian times. Their website address is: www.westmidlandspolicemuseum.co.uk/

▲ People in the slums called policemen 'crushers'.

Being arrested

When criminals were arrested they were taken to the nearest police station. After that, they were sent to a **magistrate**. A magistrate was an unpaid judge. The magistrate could sentence criminals for less-serious crimes. If the crime was serious, the criminal had to be tried in a criminal court. In court, a **jury** would decide if they were innocent or guilty.

▲ A Victorian lawyer – Henry Bodkin Poland.

Criminal trials

A trial in a criminal court was like a contest between two lawyers. One lawyer argued that the accused person was guilty. The other lawyer argued that they were innocent. At the end of the trial the judge summed up each case. The jury went away to decide whether the accused person was guilty or not. The judge announced the decision.

▲ A Victorian judge takes notes during the lawyers' arguments.

Detective work

Find out about some famous Victorian crimes from library books. Choose a crime such as burglary or murder. Imagine the speeches the lawyers on each side made during the trial. Write down some of these speeches.

▲ *This cartoon shows a rich man and a poor man in front of a magistrate. The poor man is sent to jail. The rich man pays a fine.*

▲ These pictures are of people arrested in Victorian times. The police took photographs of them. Do you think the criminals wanted to be photographed?

▼ *The picture shows Mrs Florence Maybrick on trial. She was found guilty of poisoning her husband. Only men were allowed to be on the jury.*

❧ Do you think the way an accused person looked was important in court?

❧ Why is Mrs Maybrick wearing a back dress?

The death penalty

In Victorian times murderers were given the **death penalty**. This meant they were hanged until they died. The nickname for hanging was 'being stretched'. For many years the hangings took place in public.

▼ *Charles Dickens*

Public hangings

Big crowds gathered to watch the hangings. The idea was that people would go away shocked by the hanging. They were supposed to be so scared of the punishment that they would never break the law themselves.

In 1849, the writer Charles Dickens watched a public hanging. He was upset at the number of pickpockets and ruffians in the crowd. He also felt that many people showed 'indecent delight' at the hanging.

An excited crowd watches a hanging outside Newgate Prison.

◀ *After 1868, hangings took place inside prisons. This picture shows the hanging of Louise Masset in 1900.*

🐾 Why did pickpockets enjoy public hangings?

Detective work

List the reasons why you think the government decided to stop hanging people in public?

A pickpocket at a public hanging describes his day's takings:

"I did four shillings sixpence at the hanging – two handkerchiefs, and a purse with 2 shillings in it – the best purse I ever had."

Crowded prisons

▲ *This picture shows Newgate, one of the old prisons.*

In early Victorian times, there was a rise in the number of people sent to prison. This was because there was more crime. It was also because in the past, hanging had been the punishment for more than 200 different crimes. In Victorian times, only murderers were hanged, other criminals were sent to prison.

Old prisons

People stayed in prison while they waited to go on trial. Here men, women and children were put together. After their trial they were hanged, flogged or transported (shipped) to Australia.

Incredible old hulks

Prisoners were also kept on old warships, called hulks. These ships were moored off navy bases at Woolwich, Portsmouth and Deptford. In the daytime, the prisoners worked in the dockyards. Each prisoner had to wear a leg-iron. At night they returned to the dirty, overcrowded ships.

Bad influence

Old prisons were criticised because they encouraged crime. Children and people who had done small crimes lived with and learnt from serious criminals.

Detective work

Read about a prisoner escaping from a hulk in *Great Expectations*, a novel by Charles Dickens.

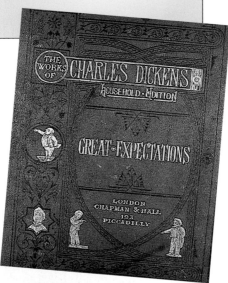

"His time is passed in the midst of a body of criminals of every class... He returns a greater adept [expert] in crime..."
Parliamentary Report, 1836

✿ Why did the prisoners wear leg-irons?

✿ How can you tell this ship is no longer used for sailing?

Getting the boat

The Victorians tried to solve the problem of overcrowded prisons. They sent some prisoners to Australia. This was called **transportation** and was nicknamed 'getting the boat'. It lasted from 1787 to 1868.

▲ *The voyage to Australia took six months. The prisoners were kept in cages most of the time.*

Life in Australia

Prisoners sent to Australia could no longer commit crimes in Britain and they were also useful in Australia. The government planned to make Australia into a British **colony**. Prisoners were needed to build towns and farm the land there. When the prisoners were freed they could settle in this new land.

The other side of the world

Around 160,000 British men, women and children were shipped to Australia. How do you think it felt to be separated from your friends and family?

✿ In 1851, gold was discovered in Australia. Do you think Australia became more popular because of this?

▲ Gold diggers celebrate.

Convicts wrote letters home to their families. This is part of a letter from a prisoner in Australia to his parents:

"We have as much to eat as we like… All a man has to do is… do his master's duty… but if he don't… they would take you to the magistrates and get 100 lashes… I am doing a great deal better than ever I was at home, only the wanting you with me."

LAST OF THE CONVICT SHIPS
OVER ONE HUNDRED YEARS OLD
RAISED FROM THE BOTTOM OF SIDNEY HARBOUR
ONCE SEEN NEVER FORGOTTEN.

CONVICT SHIP

◄ This is a photograph of the last ship used for transporting criminals to Australia.

Detective work

Discover more about transportation. Look at the Convicts to Australia website. You can find it at www.convictcentral.com/index.html.

The separate system

The Victorians tried a new way to deal with prisoners. In 1842, a prison called Pentonville was opened in London. It was built to hold around 500 male prisoners. The prisoners were kept apart in separate cells. This was called the **separate system**. They could talk only with the guards and the prison chaplain. This was supposed to stop prisoners being a bad influence on each other.

▼ *Prisoners at Pentonville met only in the exercise yard. They wore masks and uniforms.*

🐾 Why do you think the prisoners had to wear masks?

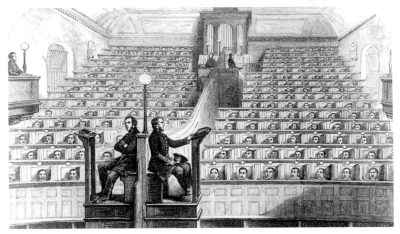

Punishing prisoners

Prisons became places where prisoners were punished. The idea was to make prison so bad that no one would ever want to go back there. One punishment was the 'treadmill'. Prisoners had to climb the steps of a big rolling drum. The prisoners turned the drum as they climbed. It was like being trapped in a machine.

▲ *This prison chapel has seats that are boxed off from each other.*

Reform

Prisoners could talk to the prison chaplain about God. It was hoped that religion might make them better people. By 1850, people realised that this did not work. Many prisoners released from Pentonville committed crime again.

✿ What was the point of turning a crank or a treadmill?

▼ *Prisoners climbing a treadmill.*

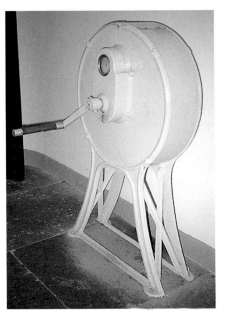

▲ *The 'crank' was another punishment. A prisoner had to turn the handle 10,000 times a day.*

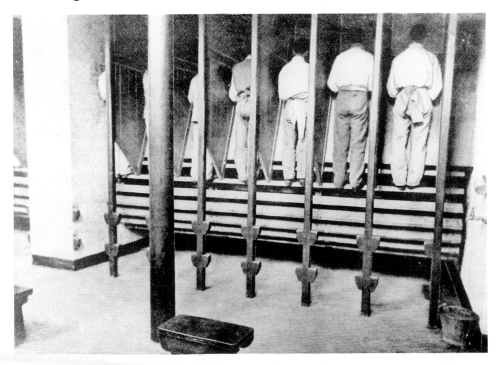

Detective work

Visit a prison museum to see what life was like for a Victorian prisoner. Places to visit include Inverary Jail, the Prison Service Museum and Lincoln Castle.

Your project

By now, you should have collected lots of evidence about Victorian crime. Now is the time to think about your project. Bring your evidence to life with your own project.

Getting started

First, you need to choose a topic to investigate. You could investigate different crimes or you may choose a punishment to investigate, such as transportation. You may want to look at the crimes that happened in your local area. Sherlock Bones has been finding out about police dogs. They were used to try to track down Jack the Ripper.

▼ A newspaper shows police dogs helping to find Jack the Ripper.

Sherlock Bones found this newspaper article about bloodhounds. He discovered it in the *Pall Mall Gazette* from October 1888. The dogs were praised for:

"keen scent, quick intelligence, patience, and power of concentration…The London police will find a good friend in the bloodhound, given patience to train him in the way he should go."

☙ A dog from the Jack the Ripper investigation appears somewhere else in this book. Can you find him?

Presentation ideas

You could make your own Victorian newspaper. Write articles and letters, draw your own cartoons and pictures. Perhaps you could be a prisoner. Write a diary entry for a day in a Victorian prison. Or you could write a policeman's notebook. Perhaps you could make notes from a day on the beat in a Victorian slum area.

▼ *In the Victorian slums people often turned to crime.*

▼ *Policemen break up a riot in Hyde Park, London.*

Glossary

arsenic A poison used to kill rats and flies. Murderers used it to poison people.

cant A secret language used by Victorian criminals.

colony A country that is ruled by another country.

cracksman Burglar or person who could break into safes.

death penalty To be killed for your crime.

fence A person that buys and sells stolen goods.

flash house A public house (pub) where criminals meet to arrange crimes and buy and sell stolen goods.

insurance money Money that is sometimes paid out when a person dies. Some people take out an insurance policy on their life with an insurance company. Their family can claim this money when they die.

jury A group of twelve men who sat in on a Victorian criminal trial. They decided whether a person was guilty or innocent.

magistrate A part-time judge. In Victorian times, only men could be magistrates. They were not paid any money for this job.

safe A metal box with a strong door and lock. It is used to hold money and precious items.

separate system A new way of running prisons that started in Victorian times. Prisoners were not allowed to mix with other prisoners. They spent most of their time alone in their cells.

slums Areas of dirty, overcrowded houses.

transportation The system of removing prisoners from Britain. They were taken by ship to Australia where they were forced to work.

Answers

page 4

☙ It was called the 'devil's acre' because people thought being there was like living in hell.

page 5

☙ The policeman is wearing a blindfold to show that he cannot find the murderer Jack the Ripper.

page 7

☙ The man on the right is keeping watch for police. The man on the left is trying to sell stolen goods to a fence.

☙ Translation of the Victorian cant: "We were shoplifting handkerchiefs when our lookout spotted a policeman and shouted, 'Get away quick!'"

page 8

☙ Poor people in Victorian times were often shorter than richer people because they did not have a healthy diet. The Artful Dodger is not very tall so we can guess that he was poor.

page 9

☙ He is trying to take the handkerchief from the suit without making the bell ring. A real pickpocket would do this without making the bells ring.

☙ The pickpocket has passed the stolen goods to the stickman. If the pickpocket is caught he will not have any stolen items on him.

page 10

☙ Burglars poisoned dogs to stop them barking.

☙ The police would not think a man dressed as a gentleman was a criminal.

page 12

✿ These men are walking back-to-back so they can watch out for garotters in all directions.

page 13

✿ This is a joke. Collars like this were found only in cartoons.

page 15

✿ Journalists wrote about the cases and this sometimes helped criminals to escape arrest.

page 17

✿ They wore top hats so they would look more like gentlemen. They also made them look taller.
✿ Helmets gave better protection than hats. They stayed on the policemen's heads if they were knocked over in a fight.

page 19

✿ The jury was made up of middle-class people and they were often on the side of people who dressed well, like themselves.
✿ Her black dress shows she is in mourning for her dead husband. She hopes this will prove her innocence.

page 21

✿ While the big crowd watched the hanging they did not notice their pockets being picked.

page 23

✿ The leg-irons stopped the prisoners swimming away from the hulk at night. They could not run away from the dockyard in the day either.
✿ The masts have been cut down.

page 25

✿ The discovery of gold in Australia made poor people want to go there, to get rich.

page 26

✿ The masks stopped prisoners getting to know each other in prison. The idea was to stop them meeting up after their release.

page 27

✿ There was no point to turning a crank or walking a treadmill. The prisoners were not doing anything useful. This made the punishment seem harsher.

page 28

✿ The bloodhound appears in the cartoon 'Is Detection a Failure?' on page 15.

Books to read

A Vile Victorian Adventure: Cradles, Castles and Curious Crimes (Horrible Histories Gory Stories) by Terry Deary (Scholastic, 2008)

Stop, Thief!: A Tale of the Victorian Police (Sparks) by Karen Wallace (Franklin Watts, 2000)

Oliver Twist (Usborne Young Reading) (Usborne, 2006)

Jammy Dodgers on the Run by Bowering Sivers (Macmillan Children's Books, 2005)

Index